Square Root of Life

$\sqrt{Life}$

Manifest
the
Ultimate Life

Sarah Davis

Fundamental techniques to:

Manifest the ultimate life

Magnify attraction,

Improve self esteem

&

Start living the life

you want

today

ISBN: 0992416515 (pbk)
ISBN-13: 978-0-9924165-1-5 (pbk)

National Library of Australia
Cataloguing-in-Publication entry:
Sarah Jayne Davis 1976

Title: Manifest the Ultimate Life / Sarah Davis.
ISBN: (paperback)
Series: Davis, Sarah J., Square root of life.
Subjects: Self-actualization (Psychology)
Conduct of life.

Dewey Number: 158.1
ISBN: 0992416515 (pbk)
ISBN-13: 978-0-9924165-1-5 (pbk.)
Self Published Edition / SQRoL Publications
Email. tosarahdavis@gmail.com
For Further information about orders: Phone: +61 422648079

Dedication

This book is dedicated to my son: Ayrton

For giving me purpose and for being my "Why".

To the readers:

We are all alike; choosing to evolve by learning how to better ourselves.

This book contains "Life" tools.

So you will be able to fulfil your goals, live the ultimate life.

and

Be the best you!

"The ultimate value of life depends

upon awareness

and the power of contemplation

rather than upon mere survival."

– Aristotle

√Life
THE SQUARE ROOT OF LIFE

It only takes one
One cell to create a living thing
One dream to create a life
One hope to return life from hopelessness
One person to save a life
One tree to sprout a thousand vines
One thought to become a reality
One book to change your thoughts
One idea to change your mindset

If you had to come up with the number of total life experiences you have encountered until today, it would be the tens of thousands.
We lead a complex existence that has endless experiences. These seemingly unrelated experiences make up who we are today, they define how we think, how we respond and react to the world around us.

The square root of life = YOU

Chapters

Interactive reading

The Square Root Of Life is taking technology and innovation to the next level in interactive book publishing.

I have had so many good responses about the QR codes, in Positive Thinking for Life, that in this book I take you to furthering your knowledge for each topic with many exciting links.

Interact and ENJOY!

All you need to do is use your tablet, iPhone, android smartphone or ipad QR scanner to scan the QR codes within the pages of this book to be redirected to the videos, opt-ins, downloads, audios and special offers. You can visit manually via your app store or Itunes store from your device to download a scanner.

Android QR Scanner App
:https://play.google.com/store/apps/details?id=me.scan.android.client

IPhone & Ipad QR Scanner App:
https://itunes.apple.com/en/app/qr-reader-for-iphone/id368494609?mt=8

If you do not have an android device, iPhone or ipad to scan the QR codes, simply view videos and audio from Sarah at:

www.squarerootoflife.com.au

Introduction

 elcome to Book 2 of the Square Root of Life Series:

Manifest the Ultimate Life.

You are about to learn the techniques needed to live the ultimate life. These are methods that improve your mindset, set you free of your limited way of living and attract whatever you desire in your heart.

Learn to manifest and attract into your life the experiences, situations, events, and people that you desire. This book will teach you tools that will enable you do just that, "match the frequency" of any imaginable situation through thoughts and feelings.

The first book, "Positive Thinking for Life," is a must pre-read to this second book. Positive thinking and feeling positive create life-changing results such as increased wealth, health, and happiness, and you need to have accomplished the habitual mental state of positive thinking before you move onto the techniques explained in this book, which go hand in hand together or, as the Law of Attraction states, it won't work for your reality.

The Law of Attraction is a natural law, like the law of gravity; if you learn how it works it will work for you. What we think and what we feel at both conscious and subconscious levels is what we attract. You will learn that by changing your thought patterns, your life will manifest in accord with what your mind wills.

And you are about to learn exactly how to do that...

Use this FREE workbook;

www.squarerootoflife.com.au/bonus

Print out use during the course of this series.

Chapter 1

Being a

Magnetic force

"You are a living magnet.
What you attract
into your life
is in harmony
with your dominant thoughts."

Brian Tracy

Magnetic Force

$\mathcal{A}$ magnetic force exists around a magnet or electrical field, and thus a magnetic force is generated electromagnetically.

Your magnetic force attracts people and experiences to you. We are like cosmic magnets. Our thoughts and feelings send out a magnetic field, and universal energy matches our attraction by giving us more of the same, resonant energy. That is why your life reflects your belief systems.

Everything is energy and energy is an attractive force, binding together to form matter as we know it. We also know that energy cannot be created or destroyed, it can only change form. I want you to accelerate your magnetic frequency, manifest vision for your life and possess the power to create and attract everything you want in your life. Using energised concentration, we can attract like a magnet.

The Law of Attraction works in a similar way to a magnet, except instead of it being an attractive force between metals, it is an attractive force between frequencies. The Law of Attraction is only practical if you become a Magnetic Person in the process.

Magnetic fields are created when an electric current flows: the greater the current, the stronger the magnetic field. You need to increase your electric flow by elevating the energy you exude. The more passionate, intense emotion you have about something, the stronger magnetic energy you are giving out.

When we concentrate on what we truly desire, we are creating emotions. If we have extremely strong emotions about something, we are transmitting strong frequencies. When we feel ecstatic or excited, we feel more electric! That is because we are actually transmitting electric frequencies, whether we realise this or not.

Positive thinking produces better energy which works in tandem with excitement or exuberance; it amplifies our magnificent attractors.

Task:

Sit for a few minutes... relax and quiet your mind.

Feel the energy field that surrounds you, allow your being to absorb into the ground, air, wind and become the universal field, now imagine you are a magnet, drawing towards you all that you desire, be at peace and allow flow.

Learn to breathe

$\mathfrak{I}$t is very important to learn to breathe through your body.

When you are feeling inspired, your body is getting plentiful amounts of oxygen, particularly to the brain. "Inspired" literally means to breathe in.

When you breathe in a correct and controlled manner, slowly and deeply, it causes your muscles to relax, heart and lungs expand, and more oxygen is carried through your body by your blood.

Your breath is a focal point for relaxing and meditating, as described in "Positive Thinking for Life". A deep, slow breath calms the mind. Whenever your thoughts are wandering off track or are becoming negative, concentrate on your breathing patterns circulating around your heart and lungs to regain focus, relaxing and emptying your mind.

Along with meditating and yoga, breathing is the focal point for the exercises; this is also the case when being magnetic.

Breathing helps to magnify your magnetic force. With each breath, feel yourself attracting and drawing towards you with each inhale; goodness and positivity, feel it flow through your entire body. Goodness being absorbed and filling your bloodstream, remaining within. As you breathe out through your nose, feel your body's toxins: stress, anxiety, and frustration flow out of your body with each exhalation.

Task:

Practice circular breathing in through your nose and out through your mouth- feel positivity being sucked in with each breath, imagine yourself as a human magnet drawing it towards you with each breathe, then negativity leaving through your body with each exhalation.

Listen & follow this centering technique video – by Yoga teacher, Reiki Master & "Best Birth Coaching" founder Rosie McCaffrey : Centering technique;

Watch these videos-

Breathing exercises   &   9 Breathing techniques

Universal Energy

𝕌niversal energy, known as divinising or spiritualising energy, has both an upward and a downward flow through the body. The upward flow is from the earth and liberates us. The downward flow of energy comes in through the crown of the head and is the energy of manifestation. Problems with chakras (points in the body, life force centers) show themselves through physical, emotional, mental and spiritual ailments within the body and mind, when this flow is clear, we get ideas and inspiration from our upper chakra's and we act on them using our lower chakras.

If there is a block in the downward flow, we can have ideas but we are unable to manifest them into the world. So having clear chakras is very important to overall wellbeing and manifesting our desires into our lives. Our body, mind and soul need to be working as one, striking a perfect, harmonic balance.

This universal energy also runs through the seven major chakras, points that govern different aspects of our body, consciousness and influence how we feel, act and manifest. A result of energetic imbalance among the chakras is an almost continuous feeling of dissatisfaction.

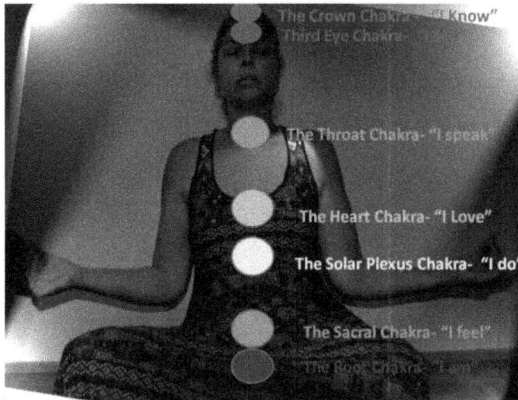

Chakra healings, clearing, balancing or cleansing results in greater self-compassion and self-love, and it removes and clears inner conflicts.

Check this site ; for <u>Chakras for Beginners</u>

Task:

Learn where your chakras are located in your body and feel light feed each whilst meditating, allow flow through each of your Chakras before you end each meditation.

Yoga

Yoga means "union" or discipline," and yoga poses can help an individual improve self-awareness, balance, and strength. Yoga has been defined as "the stilling of the changing states of the mind" or "union with the divine". The basic yoga moves involve poses and exercises which provide inner peace, radiant health, and help clear your chakras.

Yoga is a strategic mix of poses and stretching of the body held for extended breaths, improving mental endurance and physical stamina. Most are easy to do. Its focus on strength training and flexibility offers incredible benefits to your body, strengthening it from the inside-out.

Use breathing as a tool, develop slow deep rhythmic breaths whilst moving in and out of postures, use your breath to release and open tight muscles. Take your awareness to your muscle, concentrate on letting go and the muscle softening with each exhale.

These techniques have been passed down over thousands of years. Consult YouTube for instructional videos or sign up for a yoga class in your area, some links have been set up for you to scan & check out on the next page using a QR code scanner app on your smart phone or tablet.

Remember - your body is an instrument – learn to play it well and keep it in tune!

Yoga websites;

Here is a good workout at body and soul;
Or consult YouTube for instructional yoga videos

or sign up for a yoga class in your area.
Remember - your body is an instrument – learn to play it well
and keep it in tune!

Task: Look up some Yoga moves and try them at home.

Yoga poses for beginners.
*Stretch and hold the postures, with training and guidance you
will have great benefits from doing some Yoga each week.*

Aura Cleansing

Your aura is a field of subtle, luminous radiation surrounding your body – a "map of thoughts and feelings" surrounding a person with a rainbow of colour.

Cleansing your aura will remove a lifetime of accumulated negative energy, and re-energise it with positive energy (and it will also empower you to use the law of attraction).

It is recommended that you have your aura cleaned every four to six months by a professional, which is around $60-100 per visit. This helps to clean your "inner" body. Book in & spoil yourself !

The Aura is the energy field that surrounds our body, which picks up negativities from our thoughts, energies, emotions and outside sources and foreign frequencies, which have collected in our body over years and years. An Aura full of unwanted "bad" energies will prevent you from being able to transform your life, gain positive mental health and manifest correctly.

More Aura cleansing information
can be found here;

You can cleanse you Aura here ^

Task;

Hold your hand out straight in front of you with a dark background, watch the edges of your skin for a moment, can you see your own Aura – the energy waves at the edge of your silhouette? Some people can see Auras..can you?

There are home remedies that you can use in your daily and weekly routines that will assist you to <u>cleanse the aura yourself:</u>

1. Cleansing bath   1 teaspoon baking powder 1 cup of sea salt Soak in the bath for around 20 minutes, each day for 7 days. Then repeat as regularly as you like (weekly is best). This removes chemicals, toxins & negativity from the body

2. Sea salt   Swim in the ocean or saltwater lakes - this will draw out stress and negativity

   **If you don't have a bath/ live near the sea, rub sea salt all over your body before showering, removes dead skin cells and refreshes aura

3. Cold shower   Clears away negativity in your auric field, improves circulation and remove toxins and tension from your body

4. Crystals   -<u>Labradorite</u>**
   This crystal which will repair tears and leakage in your aura.
   -<u>Black tourmaline / smoky quartz</u>**
   deflects radiation and negative energy
   -<u>Amber</u>**helps strengthen your aura

**Wear as a pendant, bracelet or hold the crystal for around 20 minutes, this will last 12 hours thereafter.

5. Essential oils   -Vetiver Use; grounding and balancing, 7 drops in belly button at night

-Angelsword   repairs, dab 7 drops onto solar
plexus (below belly button)
-Fringed violet, Heals damaged and distressed
aura, dab 7 drops to solar plexus

6. Sun rays   -Sunshine - is known to expand and feed your aura,
fuels you with energy, nourishes senses
and grounds you

7. White sage   -Smudging clears out and dissolves
negative blockages and energies. Burn
some white sage it's a room so that it fills
with smoke and remain in the room, or
use a sage stick and use your hand direct
it over your body, also use through your
home to remove negative energies at
home

Task:
Make the time to do at least one of the above tasks weekly,
the more the merrier.
Make it a ritual for your weekly bath to add baking powder and
sea salt, get some crystals and embrace cleansing your aura

Some natural remedies are mind blowing...

To learn more about all different healing affects of crystals ;
That Crystal site:

To learn more about essential oil benefits

Chapter 2

Transmitting

Frequency

"What we call the 'world' and the 'universe' is only one frequency range in an infinite number

sharing the same space.

The inter-dimensional entities

I write about

are able to move between

these frequencies or dimensions

and manipulate our lives"

David Icke

Spirit Guides

$\mathfrak{J}$ ust imagine... you are source energy, part of a greater puzzle, part of an ineffable, unfathomable universal consciousness. Now imagine that there is an adjoining spirit connected to us on a subconscious level who may really be just source energy which we know as spirit.

Spirits could be deceased family members, saints, gods, angels, ascended masters, masters in certain areas here to help you (who especially help to enable you to fulfill your earthly mission), souls who walk among us, guardian angels who are the most enlightened spirits, or normal kindred spirits, members of your "soul" family who are connected to us on a level higher than consciousness and beyond this earth.

Advanced spiritual energy forms teach, guide, support or heal us along our journey through life. We are spiritual energy with a human physical body, living on earth's plane, here for many different purposes. Our spirit guides are from the other side, from the realm of spirit or heaven (whichever terminology resonates with you: it is all one place.)

Look into enlisting the help of your spirit guides here.

There are many different guides with you at any one time. You do not have to be a psychic to connect with them, see their work or feel their presence. Once you have the desire to connect, with practice and patience your guides will manifest themselves to you in many different forms and their assistance can be practical or spiritual in nature. It takes a lot of practice to intentionally connect with your spirit guides but you can connect in many ways, the most popular being through meditation, they connect to you mainly through your intuition, gut feelings, signs such as words repeating in your daily travels that resonate with you on a topic you are seeking advice on. You can also see a professional psychic.

Spirit guides keep a connection to your higher self and your soul's purpose, gently guiding you to keep you on track toward your higher purpose, and "guiding" you intuitively with instinctive nudges in the right direction. They will hook up people, information, resources, money, etc. to help you reach your goals.

We only want to attract reliable, enlightened spirit guides. The more receptive you are to your guide the more guidance, support and love your guide will give you.

Task:

By saying "I invite wise and loving spirit guides and angels to be with me now" each morning while you wake and asking for their guidance shows your intention and desire to attract.

This way, your guides are able to help you even more.

Here are more sites with information that may help you enlist their help;

Spirit guides & Angels

Trusting your spirit guides

Meet your spirit guides-

Guided meditation video

Angel contact video

- Ask your spirit guides to protect you with the greatest love and light
- Invite them into your life and give them permission to be with you
- Ask them for a sign of their presence
- Ask your spirit guides for whatever you need assistance with
- Thank them for being with you and guiding you
- Ask them for their name and age, even what they look like!
- Ask your guide for any messages, gifts or advise they may have for you
- Ask them what type of guide they are
- Ask them how long they have been with you
- Ask for a golden sphere of love, light and protection to come into your body
- Ask them to be closer to you

If you are unable to connect immediately, relax, have patience and practice your ability to connect. The best way to do so is through meditation: clear your mind, quiet your thoughts, and open yourself to receive the truth that will manifest in you.

Go and meet with a medium that will connect for you and tell you who is around you and any messages they may have. This may help facilitate future connections.

Take part in a tarot reading, during which your spirit guides will connect with you through the cards. Let them connect with you, answer your questions; allow them to fulfill their mission and purpose.

Keep all of your senses open: stay tuned to "coincidences", watch for repetition they are your spirit guides trying to get through.

They are always by your side, have never left you and are waiting to re-establish communication. Establish a working relationship with them and connect with them regularly.

Task

Get a set of Tarot cards and clear your mind as you shuffle and ask one question: whichever card "falls" out of the pack is no accident. Your spirit guides work in mysterious ways. Ask a question and let them the answer with the card, if you are not comfortable doing it yourself book a reading – you may be pleasantly surprised.

Here is a link about Tarot for beginners

Each time you connect with your guides – write it down in a journal or note book. Some day's it's hard to remember what we ate for lunch the previous day. By writing down the messages from your guides you will be able to refer back to them, it will help you to remember them and you may get greater meaning at a later date

List what you would like to ask them before you connect.

Be Positive

$\mathcal{T}$he mind control chapter (Chapter 1 of Positive Thinking for Life, book 1 of the Square Root of Life series) was a lesson in removing your negative thoughts. Practice seeing thoughts that contradict what feeling you would like, view the thought and see it fade away, or hold it out and let go of it... This allows you to be aware of how your mind is working.

We often ponder experiences when we were wronged or victimised, but we must let go, forgive and move forward.

Consult the first book in this series "Positive Thinking for Life" for more information on the ability to control your thoughts and removing negativity.

There is a saying, "lye with dogs and you get fleas". Are you surrounding yourself with people that put you down or push you up? Are your associates positive and good to be around, or do you need to let go of a few negative influences in your life?

Some may be even family or friends you've had since childhood. But if you don't look around at whom you are with and how they are, you will get knocked off your perch over and over again. You don't have to sever contact entirely, but understand in order for you to evolve and progress as an evolved person; you may need to spend more time with the people that bring out your best, make your smile and dwell on the good in life. See others for what they are, accept "that" is who they are and concentrate on living a better life: remove all negative influences, as they will "rub off" onto you!!

Positivity is a *chosen* state of mind, one we must learn to cultivate. Life experiences are the result of habitual and predominant thoughts. Thus, look for the bright side to anything and everything.(Perform the tasks in book 1 "Positive Thinking for Life" to obtain the right mental attitude.)

After doing it long enough (4-6 weeks consistently), it will become habitual. Even when we have a bad experience, they are valuable; choose what part of the experience to focus on: this is how we learn and grow as spiritual beings. Smile and think about your "cue", where you are going and your goals, not what you are experiencing. Take time out to recharge and regain your perspective.

Here's an article;

7 negative influences to remove from your life- especially with today's technology and social media- more negative influences can come from the internet interaction we have than we realise.

Use the law of attraction, remembering that our positive and negative thoughts are like magnets, and that we attract whatever occupies our thoughts.

Task:

Do something nice for someone else, if it's unexpected they will really appreciate you and in turn you will feel great satisfaction.

Try to do at least one good deed daily - it's better than an apple a day!

Karma

Karma is the concept of an "action" or "deed" that causes an entire cycle of cause and effect. Whatever you do comes back to you, supposedly tenfold.

It can be good or bad karma, depending on the action or deed done. Action performed in "free will" in turn cause a reaction.

The theory behind Karma can be found here;

This is a fundamental law of the universe. "The act" is any kind of intentional action; mental, verbal or physical. The law states whether "thought, word or deed" the action taken constitutes karma.

Using this knowledge, decide to do good deeds for others, perform some sort of charity work, help others in their time of need, and do so selflessly (meaning that you do not expect anything in return). You will be a creator of your own karma.

We are the result of what we were, what we thought and the action we have taken. We can change our circumstance now by changing and becoming a person that works in the happiness and wellbeing of others, changing the cause and effect of your life.

Karma is like a seed; "we reap what we sow", somewhere, at some time in the future.

Don't be ignorant of the greater power at work; use it to manifest all good things in your life by working with these laws. We are constantly changing entities that can be the reaper of the fruits we sow!

Internalize this law, manifest it in your deeds and actions, and cultivate it in your daily life. The future is in your hands!!!

Try to make every effort to do one good deed a day, by doing this your intent will be sending out and transmitting frequencies of enthusiasm, love and kindness for the universe, overtime your life will flourish.

Task   (chapter 9 – in the workbook)

Whatever you do will have an equal or greater reaction, make everything you do positive.

Write down 10 things that you could do each day that would send positive karma back to you

Wave or smile as you greet people, compliment someone, appreciate kindness, donate something, help someone in need.

Removing EGO

hen we try to force things that aren't going our way- it is more the work of our ego. If your desire does not manifest within *your* timeframe negativity towards the actions may develop.

To constantly look towards helping others and doing good deeds, you are removing your ego from the equation. Using Karma as a mental tool, you are residing to the belief of the circle of action and reaction, this will create more of your desires to unfold unto you and you will find that more "coincidences" of good fortune will come to you.

To feel that you are being "selfish" to request or desire abundance in your life is also part of your ego. There is no reason for you to feel ashamed of wanting things. To remove your egos negativity with the art of giving and helping, you will reinforce that you do deserve to live a life of abundance and that you are worthy to receive these desires.
When you radiate positivity and assist others to receive happiness through your deeds and actions, you will facilitate an attitude of deserving abundance, enabling yourself to accept all blessings that you manifest into your life.

You are engaging a path to trust yourself, knowing that you are worthy of better things and being able to attract and manifest in your world. You will be more aware of your higher self, knowing that you are not separate from your environment, that you are part of frequency within the environment which gives you the power to be able to manifest and attract what your heart desires from this world.

^ David Icke.com gives a detailed technique to remove ego

Love what you do

𝕿ransmitting the right frequency has a lot to do with your current mood or emotional state. The only way to do great things is to "do what you love" … but I don't mean go and look for a new job, start from where you are and what you have in your life today.

Look at your current state, job, relationships, etc., and find the love that exists therein! Focus on the best parts. You may not like your job now, but maybe you have great workmates. Consider even the little things that you enjoy: the lunch break, using the photocopier, the menial but important tasks. There is boundless beauty caught up in the little things in this world. Focus on whatever gives you that "satisfied to the soul" feeling, and find it!

The only way you can create more of the more is to be in it NOW. When you have time to yourself, or make time for yourself do the things you love: write a poem, draw a picture, take your dog on a nature walk, relax and become one with the earth: breathe through your body, feel the universe's energy as it continually flows.

Switch off when people are talking about things that don't agree with your inner balance, use your mind to remove negatives around you and use your "cue"(your "bliss" moment, outlined in book 1, chapter 1 in "Positive Thinking for Life") to take you somewhere that replenishes your soul. Imagine you are somewhere else – anywhere. Just have the feeling of love abundant in your life and you will be sending the right frequency to the universe.

When you are "in love" with someone, nothing else matters; the sky could be falling down but the only thing you feel are those butterflies in the stomach, the joyful romantic elation, the constant glow you radiate thinking about your new love. That is where you need to be with your everyday actions: work, home or socially.

You will be unlocking the key and activating the unlimited power that lies with you. Creating confidence and being in love with your life and yourself will attract exactly that; in turn, people around you will love to be with you; love your company; workmates will love working with you.

You're immediately more attractive to everyone around you simply because it feels good to be around you. By understanding and following this simple rule, the universe will align your life around the frequency you transmit and you will be amazed at what you manifest.

Task;   *(chapter 9 in the workbook)*

Write down five things that you love about each of the following topics (or create your own):

Partner, Children, Work, Friends, Parents, Home, Holidays, Neighbours, Suburb, Pets

Be Content

𝔄ccept your imperfections and don't make comparisons

The Bible clearly teaches us to "be content" no matter what our circumstances are. In Philippians 4:11, Paul said, *"I have learned in whatsoever state I am in therewith to be content."* Until God bring change, it doesn't say don't want change, but *"satisfied to the point where you are not disturbed or disquieted" "continue to make God aware of what you want".* Philippians 4:6-7

So how can you practice contentment?

• Want what you have. Practice basic appreciation and gratitude. Don't take your possessions for granted. Acknowledge every day one thing that improves your life. Make a list of things you are grateful to have in your life.

• Don't make comparisons to others. Concentrate on what you are that makes you different from the rest. What makes you unique? We all have God-given talents or gifts; embrace the fact that you are different and appreciate your uniqueness.

• Accept your imperfections and what you may be lacking. We all have shortcomings or faults, but none of these matter. What matters is that you enjoy what you have. Be happy and proud that you are different.

Task

3 ways to be content;

Change your perspective! Close your eyes and take some deep breaths. Focus on being in the moment and you'll feel all of your worries melt away. Feel the emotion of gratitude for your life.

Be grateful for what you have; *Use the task in chapter 6- such as a gratitude diary. Spend more time in nature or doing the "free" things in life ie; take your child to the swings, or walking your dog along the river*

Appreciate the little things ; *Be thankful for everything small and large - even the clean air you breathe*

Chapter 3

Attraction

and

Manifesting

"If your ruling mental state
is upward bound, that is,
aspiring, harmonious, and positive,
all your forces will be
directed into constructive channels;
but if your state of mind is downward
in tendency, that is, discordant and
negative, then almost all your forces
will be misdirected."

–Raymond Holliwell

Be one with the universe

$\mathcal{A}$waken new thought at every turn.

Focus on delight and only choose to see the goodness that surrounds you at any given time.

You have the ability to manifest and attract all that you desire. Becoming aware of your higher self, knowing you are limitless and by acknowledging that you are part of the infinite energy of the universe, the spirit energy that lies within, lies within all things created, eternally.

The consensus is that we all have a soul or a spirit-form within. This higher self allows us to co-create with God: we can be or allow anything we desire into our lives, we do this through unseen waves of energy. It is more than within you: it *is* you!

Manifesting is about attracting what is already part of you on a spiritual level. If you are able to see yourself as part of what you desire or to becoming one with that you desire- the feeling of having it and tuning into divine energy associated around your desire will turn it into your reality.

Be compassionate to those around you, do not judge, see them as source energy like yourself, as individuals who may be at a different stage of their spiritual evolvement.

Be at peace; do not make positive thinking a "chore". You need to be in an ebb-and-flow frame of mind, like the John Lennon song "Let It Be". Just allow for the course of the universe to unfold as you know it will, relax and know that what is unfolding is right for you and do not stress or try to predict what lies ahead, just set the positives in your everyday life and positives will surround you.

The whole purpose of being one with the universe is to unfold with no resistance: like the grass grows, the wind blows and the ocean flows.

The main point when manifesting and attracting goodness of all kinds into your life is not to try to "force" your requests. It is like a set-and-forget diary reminder: you're not to constantly request for things to arrive into your life, like a new car, watch, etc. and then forever look for them to come, as that actually prevents their arrival!

You need to constantly appreciate what you have for more to come forth. You need to see the abundance around you today in order for abundance to continue to surround you and expand.

Spending a few minutes each day to visualise what you would like to have in your life, and then appreciate everything you do have for the rest of the day.

Imagine that a person wants lots of money in order to be ultimately happy, or so they think, and they come into the wealth. Yet they still don't have the happiness they assumed it would bring. The truth is... happiness, abundance, wealth and fulfillment starts within, the way the law of attraction works is "the more/the more," so you need to *feel* content first to become content. You need to *feel* happy all of the time to live a happy life. Consequently, if you feel happy, you will already be living a happy life and then the universe will reward you and give you more that makes you happy!!

Trust and belief coincide with manifesting; you must trust yourself to create the life you truly desire. The evidence of trust is apparent when what you think, feel and do are in balance and in harmony. You need to be at peace knowing that all will unfold to you at the right time, and believe that what you seek is on its way.

When you let go, surrender to the knowledge that all will be well you are following the path you have elected for yourself, allowing divine guidance when choosing your actions you will co-create your existence.

Task:

Focus your mind in an aspirational, harmonious, positive energy way. Look and actually see the beauty that lies in every view.

See whatever resonates passion, delight and happiness with you... continually see in an upward mental state.

17 Second Rule

$\mathfrak{T}$est the 17 second rule ... Why is it a rule?

Your mind will acknowledge 17 seconds of manifesting something. But if you only manifest for 8 seconds (for example), your brain will automatically "dump" on the creation for 8 seconds after, therefore it will become void and pointless.

While if you make sure it is a 17-second manifestation of what your heart desires, it will actually tire your brain, which will then move onto other thoughts. It's just a brain game!

It could be a placebo effect, your subconscious *now* knows that if it manifests for 17 seconds, it will create in your dimension without diluting the idea, and your brain will follow your beliefs. It's a 17 second paradigm!

Here is a video link to guide you more about this rule

 - Test it out!

Task

Manifest small events or objects into your immediate reality using the 17 second rule.

> *1;   Each time you go to the shopping centre, imagine the car space you want. For 17 seconds see the car space, see yourself pulling into it, park there in your mind.*

When you arrive at the car park, that space will be available to you, or someone will move out of the desired space within a few minutes.

TEST IT – Do it each time you go to park and see the Law of Attraction working for you.

If you are immediately saying to yourself "oh that won't work" ... it won't !!

2: Spend 17 seconds each day manifesting a smile on a stranger, or a cup of coffee, or whatever small thing you think is achievable ...See it, hold it, smell it.

Imagine it within your possession and then go through your day and see where it appears. Do it every day or every time you go somewhere or park somewhere. You will be surprised!

Having It NOW

$\mathbb{T}$his is a 20 minute workshop that you should try to fit in every day before you go to sleep, it will enhance your dreams and manifest everything you desire.

You need to imagine everything you desire. In your reality, holding it in your possession or being with whatever it may be. Relish in the feelings of having it *now*; it is already part of your reality.

What would that feel like?

How happy would you be?

Examine every angle of it, see yourself holding or touching it. Visualise it as realistically and vividly as you can.

During the day, see nice things that you love. A hot car that drives past, or clothes that appeal to you, or a piece of jewelry in a shop window, and put it in your "workshop mental toolbox".

Save that image for the 20 min workshop and visualise that item in your possession.

That will help instill gratitude time you see something you like, as you have something new for your workshop to visualise. It will make you appreciate all the nice things that surround you, and the best thing is that more you find for your "mental toolbox," the faster you are manifesting it into your reality as you are appreciating more things throughout the day.

Task   (chapter 10 in the workbook)

- *When you are out and about next, make a metal note of everything that you see that makes you say, "oh, that's nice"*

- *Get as many "nice" things as you can for the workshop that night.*
- *Write them in your journal if you like to help you remember your tools!*
- *Before you go to sleep, lie down and relax your breathing and imagine your tool box is full of all the lovely things you have seen and imagine having them: their colour, their feel, their smell, what you would do with them, how you would look after them...*
- *For around 20 minutes, keep them vividly in your mind until they become part of your imagined reality.*

Do this every night before you fall asleep for at least 6-8 weeks or approximately 66 days for the average person, that way you are habitualising appreciating nice things and habitualising manifesting each night!!

Analyse current surrounds

𝕱eel the sun shining down upon you. Feel the warmth. Close your eyes and take three slow deep breaths. Inhale. Exhale. Inhale. Exhale. Inhale. Exhale. Feel your connection to the source of the universe. Feel good?

Of course, sometimes you are surrounded by bad frequencies or surroundings that diminish your efforts of attraction and deplete your own energy. You need to remove negatives from your everyday life to be able to be able to harness the full power of attraction.

Take a moment to work out what in your immediate surrounds does not align you with the greater energies of peace and prosperity: pictures, wall hangings, books and sometimes your acquaintances.

Know that everything in the universe has its own energy, obviously plants and living matter has a greater energy than say an item, but pictures, photos and paintings can also give off or create energies that reside with you.

If you are want a life of abundance, re-evaluate what you have hanging on the walls, or items that you may have lying around; are they creating positivity when you look at them or are they draining??

To be in the feeling of abundance the majority of the time, hang pictures of mansions, beaches, photos of the special memories or occasions that you were in your element, which make you feel "bliss" when you see them.

Surround yourself with lovely things to create an ongoing positive feeling whenever you enter each room, even your desk at work!

Task

Go through your current photos, pictures, paintings and ornaments; arrange them all with your current "bliss" items.

Look for things that you feel "excited" to see. Remove any "blasé" items in which you have no interest or which don't provoke any emotional resonance.

Create spaces around you that you enjoy and give you a positive feeling.

This will help you hold onto your good feelings and will create manifesting space around you, ensuring you remain in a powerful feeling of having great abundance now!

"Appreciation is the highest
form of prayer,
for it acknowledges
the presence of good
wherever you shine the light
of your thankful thoughts"

- Alan Cohen

Chapter 6

Appreciation

and

Gratitude

"Remember to be grateful
in all things that come your way.
They are coming as a blessing
or to lift you
to receive a blessing."

Rev Michael Bernard
Beckwith

Stop-Check (s)

An effective technique is to do a "stop-check". It will help with negative thoughts and worry, also known as "thought stopping".

In this technique you simply recognise that you are not mentally in a place of peace and harmony.

When you are losing track of your thoughts or find yourself spiraling into a negative emotion, a "stop-check" will help you reestablish control.

A "stop-check" consists of replacing the thought with a positive one.

- Identify when you are have a negative thought
- Stop everything you are doing 1 – 10 seconds
- Breathe deeply (also relieves stress and anxiety)
- Take a moment to calm your mind, let it go blank
- Close your eyes if you can
- Think of something that you are grateful for
- Consume yourself with the thought of appreciation
- Be *really* grateful with your whole being
- Say "thank you" in your mind

This technique serves to bring more appreciation into your life and helps resolve momentary lapses of negativity.

This is a quick re-structure of your thoughts when you only have a moment to collect them.

It's like counting from 1-10, only this has a more positive effect and being grateful in this moment helps you to reassess the stress.

It is preferred that if you have a couple of minutes to address the bad thought or feeling, you can go back to book 1, chapter 2 and perform a "Reset" technique, but if you need to quickly change your thought track and are hurriedly moving about your day, this brief appreciation technique will assist you quieting your mind.

Task:

Practice a "stop-check" momentarily right now... Focus on an idea which stimulates gratitude.

Try to use this technique a few times each day to bring you into an appreciative emotional state. This will enhance your attraction frequency.

Openly Appreciate

𝕿his is a very mindful task that you will need to learn. It is a skill that instantly changes your attitude, but without sincere appreciation it is meaningless.

Learning to appreciate everything around you including yourself is quite uncomfortable at first. You may feel that you are not quiet genuine, this is why you need to break down the basics of feeling appreciative.

Take a few moments each day to notice what is around you

- Imagine a world without them/it!
- Imagine that you didn't have _____ around you
- Be happy that you do have a world with _____ in it
- Tell someone how you appreciate them in your life
- Express genuine thanks when someone does something for you
- Tell people *why* you appreciate them
- Verbalise your appreciation
- Ask and tell yourself each day; what can you be proud of?
- Take a deep breath and say "Thank you" in your mind and smile

As with the saying "Is your glass half full or half empty?" It is the way that you look at the world that changes your outlook from within that in turn will change your outer experiences.

Everything that you encounter has a positive and negative balance when you are in an even mind plateau, you may not have any thoughts: when you are negative you will only see the negative and when, and when you are in a positive emotion, you will see beauty in anything and everything...

Task (Chapter 11 in the workbook)

Write down everything that you are grateful for.

Try to evaluate every aspect of your life today and what you encounter daily and find the positive in each and write what you are most grateful for.

Forgive and be grateful?

One of the hardest traits to acquire is how to forgive and let go, especially in light of extremely harsh experiences.

You may have been cheated on by your spouse, they walked out and left, you may have had a close person steal from you or rip you off, or your best friend betrayed you. Such events may have caused extreme emotional pain and torment.

In the midst of such misfortunes, your emotions are in a whirlwind of pain, deceit and anger, which travels through every part of your entire being. Hatred and anger emotions are the most damaging to you, not the person that may or may not be affected by their actions, and this fuels the flames. When this is fresh in your current reality it is very hard to see any good come of what has happened.

However, when you slowly come to terms with the fact that "they choose" to do what they have done, you need to start with forgiving YOURSELF first! Understanding that a humans natural reaction to these types of event is to first scream "why" and then to point at themselves "How could I : let this happen/ be so stupid/not seen the signs/trust them."

You may be a victim, but don't *become* a victim by internalizing this fact! You did not intend for this to happen; *they* did! Sometimes we are entrapped by other people's actions towards us and fail to see what good has or could come out of it.

Every event that has happened has brought you to point that you are at today, has made you who you are today and will shape the rest of your days. It can be as positive or negative as you allow it to be, so take control today and release them.

Task   (Chapter 12 in the workbook)

Write down all of the major difficulties that you have faced along your journey until now.

Leave a few lines between each, and make a list of things that have affected you to your core!

Take a moment and go though each event with appreciation in mind:

What have you learnt?

What positive things have happened since as a result?

Who have you met due to this occurring?

What path has this event opened up to you?

What wouldn't be in your life today, had it not been the way it eventuated? i.e. your children, your new job, your new partner Work out for yourself;

What you have to be appreciative about from the event occurring then for each one release gratitude for you now understand why you now have___ and acknowledge in your mind that you forgive as ___would not have occurred and you are grateful for the event.

- *This will shift your perception and release the resentment and transform the experience.*

Gratitude Diary

This is not an ordinary diary, but rather a tool for inspiration and growth on your journey to enlightenment.

It will heighten your thoughts of gratitude and love, will change your state of being and excel you into prosperity.

When you give thanks verbally, mentally and spiritually, you become a happier individual in the life you lead today. Writing it down or noting exactly what you are grateful for on a regular occasion forces you to pay attention to all of the good things in life as you ebb and flow through your thoughts.

There is no right way or wrong way, but don't make it a chore! You don't *have to* write in it every day or faithfully keep a journal next to your bed, such that it becomes a burden you feel you *must* write in everyday! Rather, make it as pleasurable and simple as possible.

Download an app that triggers you to think about what has occurred that you are grateful for as various times or days. With today's Smartphone's, you can program it to automatically pop up and ask for 3 things you are grateful, it is quick and simple and a pleasure to read as the list of previous entries pop up on the screen. Remember that if you lose your phone or it is cleared of memory, you will no longer have the information at hand- so writing them in a book will prevent this occurring.

A gratitude diary is a very powerful tool that keeps you in a grateful and positive state of mind.

Thankfulness is an attitude that needs to be practiced and developed. Be grateful for what you have in your life, and for yourself:

What do you appreciate about *you*?

Give thanks for anything that you appreciate in your life.

Task

Go to your app store and download a gratitude journal, or try the Law of Attraction app "Secret of Happiness", an easy to use simple reminder app that will help you adhere to these daily practices.

Or if you prefer get a small note book and start a gratitude diary. Note that it is better to find new things to be grateful for rather than repeat them.

Lookout for "The Gratitude diary" and "My Life Planner" in the Square Root of Life - series range.

Chapter 7

Daily and Lifetime Intention

"Repetition of the same thought

or physical action

develops into a habit

which,

repeated frequently enough,

becomes an automatic reflex."

-Norman Vincent Peale

Building and breaking habits

$\mathfrak{R}$epetition is one of the most important tools when working with the Law of Attraction.

It is the key to change, form habits, create beliefs and experience a new *you*.

You may have read over and over again what the Law of Attraction actually is, but without absorbing the knowledge and learning how to implement it in your life, the knowledge remains ineffective.

Each chapter has given you tasks to perform as you have continued through these books; they are tasks that through repetition will develop as reflexes or habits of the mind. Learning how to implement each task is to simply repeat it until it becomes second nature.

Most habits are formed unknowingly, especially negative ones that emerge as a result of trauma or some other negative experience. The depression that thereby arises occurs automatically, through repetition, as you have been in that frame of thought for a period of time and they tend to occur subconsciously.

It is commonly thought that it takes 21 days to form or break a habit, but THIS IS INCORRECT! Statistics from research and studies of many different types and ages of people have proven to show that the timeframe can vary.

Many people get really down on themselves, thinking that 21 days breaks or makes a habit and feel quite deflated when this does not occur for them.

On average, habit forming or breaking took 66 days, with some forming a habit in 18 days, some taking longer,
as many as 84 days. (PsychCentral.com, World of Psychology)

So let's take 66 days as the benchmark.

Task
Set your timeframe for habitual change: "66 days" from today.

Look back at the chapters which entail tasks of the mind to be performed, such as the "Freeze Frame" "Stop-Check" "17 second rule" and make an effort to do these tasks multiple times daily for 66 days, in-order for your mind to habitually do them.

If needed, set them as a multiple reminder on your phone.

It's your time

"Our actions are the results

of our intentions

and our intelligence"

- E. Stanley Jones

Once you set about to rewire your brain, believe that you are on your way to living a different and more abundant life. Positive thinking is crucial, but only through your actions can you achieve these results.

Keep your word – to yourself. It is much harder to tell someone you will do something and then to not follow through and stand by what you say, but when you are only answerable to yourself, it's easy not to follow through. Yet, if your action don't match your words you lose control of your life, it will chip away at your sense of self and decrease your power. Doing what you say you will do is the cornerstone of integrity, even with yourself.

The most common reason that people don't follow through with their original desire for change is that they get "blasé" about the reason why they are doing it, lose the ability to manifest and don't see any fruition of their highest dreams or desires. Be true to you!

Task

Continually "bask in the glory" of where you see yourself next year, in 5 years, 10 years or more. Use the "20-minute workshop" before you fall asleep each night and remind yourself what you want in life, this will help keep you interested in improving your life and habituating a new way of thinking.

Make a list of "promises" to yourself of how you will improve yourself and revise regularly to ensure you keep your promise to yourself.

Use affirmations & motivation cues or cards daily to inspire you

If you would like to purchase "The Divinity Cards" in this range

1. *Affirmations cards – 78 daily cards, large size deck*
2. *Motivation & Inspirations – 78 daily cards – Large size*

> Affirmations

> Motivation /Inspiration

Set your intentions

"You are what your deepest desire is.
As your desire is, so is your intention.
As your intention is, so is your will.
As your will is, so is your deed.
As your deed is, so is your destiny."- Deepak
Chopra

Your intentions will help you take greater control of where your life is going and assist you to manifest your dreams. But first, you must have a plan or purpose and set your mind to it. To begin manifesting your desires, the first step is to set your intentions.

You need to be clear about what you want to change: write it down and work out how you will get to that result.

By setting an intention, you are setting your focus on the starting point for change. Everything that happens in the universe starts with intention.

To set an intention is to plant a seed in your mind and heart. Once you know what you want or where you want to be, intending it also requires some work. Like a seed sprouting, you need to water your intentions daily to see them come to fruition

"Our bodies are our gardens to which

our wills are gardeners."

—William Shakespeare

Task

Each day start with a little intention: intend to have a great day, intend to learn something new today, intend to be nice to everyone you come into contact with, intend to take a small step each day towards improving yourself.

Write down a list of intentions that you want to see come to fruition, this will give you guidance.

"You are a child of the universe,
no less than the trees and the stars;
you have a right to be here.
And whether or not it is clear to you,
no doubt the universe is unfolding

as it should."

-Max Ehrmann

Chapter 12

The

Action

Process

"A real decision is measured

by the fact that

you've taken a new action.

If there's no action,

you haven't truly decided."

-Tony Robbins

Be enlightened

"The more you trust your intuition, the more empowered you become, the stronger you become, and the happier you become." - Gisele Bundchen

The visual picture you have in your mind will assist you to know that the creative energy is flowing through you - source energy that connect you with everything living. Your thoughts are creative actions; it is all about what you will become.

Recognising and embracing your inherent self-worth opens your life to boundless possibilities. Accept yourself without complaint; compliment yourself for being who you are. You are created in God's image – you are a creator, God is within you, we are all God's children. Accept his divine energy that flows through you and all creation, and be aware of the power that lies within you. Be at peace in knowing that all of creation is in turn connected; accept total responsibility for yourself so that you are in a position of attracting and receiving the object of your desires.

Understand that you need to be in harmony with your thoughts, feelings and behavior in order to become enlightened.

How do you know if you are "enlightened"? As you go along this journey, you will come to notice small changes in yourself and around you. Are you experiencing spiritual awareness? How do you know?

10 common signs:

- Sleep patterns change:
  you feel more restless but have more energy
  This will adjust in time, get used to it and don't worry

- Flashes of great inspiration/ thoughts and creativity,
  tingles and vibration felt around head and ears, tingles or
  crawling sensations on your scalp.
  This is the crown chakra and divine energy flowing in

- Sudden waves of emotion: feeling sad, lonely, happy for no reason
  Blocked emotions can come out from the heart chakra,
  acknowledge them, let them rise and let go with love

- Old issues keep coming back and sometimes you may feel lost
  You may will face old issues multiple times, as you mentally
  deal with the torment you are doing necessary cleansing until
  they lye resolved within

- Your physical body can change and your eating habits become
  healthier

  Your vibration will rise as you surrender with unconditional
  love

- Your senses increase and you become more aware of subtle
  energies
  You may see sparkles of light or shadows; movement
  in the corners of your eyes, you will also be aware of a

"someone," a sense around you, humming in your ears, fleeting smells or hearing your name called! These are your spirit guides, here to help you: but you are in charge

- You see the world with new loving eyes, and are at one with everything

Your awareness continually expands: be compassionate and gentle, some bad days will still happen; be gentle with yourself. Keep the flow

- You desire more and break free of old habits and restrictive patterns

You are clearing out the old to make room for the new -have courage and embrace it

- You notice more signs speaking to you on a profound level

They have great meaning to you as your awareness blossoms

- Synchronicity flows faster

Events flow, on the right path there are no limits to the "coincidences" that come, feel the message and trust your intuition

Here's a link to help with enlightenment;

and qualities of an enlightened person;

Task

Keep notes on little things that you notice occurring, and be aware that you are not alone and divine energies connect with you on many levels – life is a learning process.

As you progress through your growing spiritual awareness and blossoming enlightenment, write how your life is changing.

Incorporate into your life

$\mathfrak{D}$on't sweat the big stuff?.. It may seem that there are so many tasks to do daily that you will not be able to incorporate all of the new ways of thinking into your day. Take a breath and take it slowly!

Once you have the "will" for change, now that you have the mind tools and techniques to make the change, once you incorporate it into daily life, everything will fall into place.

WASS'UP YoL

Wake up   Look up at your inspiration
(vision board or visual prompt)
– spend two minutes imagining your desire.
Let your mind be consumed with the visuals
produced by imagining having it now and
consume yourself with the visuals, *feel* how it will
feel.

Admire   Think of all the wonderful things the future holds
and how amazing your life will be
- Take an extra two minutes in bed before you
start the day to set your intentions

Stand up   As soon as you get out of bed, be grateful – bask
in appreciation for what you have *now*
- As you get ready; toilet, teeth, shower, etc.,
keep your appreciation thoughts going. Feel how
lucky you are!

Set off	Look for amazing things as you wander through your day: for the "workshop" and your appreciation observations - Remember to find things that appeal to you (desire) and amaze you (thank for)
U-Turn	For every negative thought that comes into your head: freeze frame, stop-check, be mindful - Use your emotional guidance to remind you to stop thinking negatively and use your "cue"
Power	Feel the flow of energies around you, smile, and sing to yourself to keep the momentum - Be in abundance and content throughout your day feel your power and energies excelling
You can	Affirmations thoughts throughout the day will confirm and affirm your intentions and help your mindset - Know you can, feel you can, be all you can, each and everyday
Observe	Watch around you as great things and situations happen, be thankful straightaway - Even a traffic light that's green just for you: say "thank you, traffic god! "Have fun with it
Laugh	Laugh at the new world you have created, enjoy your new found happiness and always smile

Remember; WASS'UP YoL – I'm feeling good!!!
(WASS'UP YO'L is each letter from the list)

"WASS'UP YoL" ask yourself, answer "I'm feeling good," and say it to yourself in any accent you like, as long as you smile and laugh throughout your day, this will help you to remember the intention you have for each new day.

As you go to sleep each day do a "workshop" in your mind for 20min, bring all of the admired things you noticed that day into your visualisation and be there!

Task
Write out the "wass'up Yol" task list into your book and keep a list on you in your wallet to remind or write it in your diary so you can always view what is required for 66 days or until it becomes a habitual process.

"A leaf from your own book"

$\mathfrak{A}$s YOU KNOW HOW the saying goes, but now you can now take a leaf from your own book!

Now you have a workbook/ journal which that has worked out and tackled all of the troubles and woes that you were facing...

This book has chronicled your deepest desires, explored inner beliefs, and spelled out your greatest challenges as you progressed through each chapter.

Re-read the chapters and re-do the tasks. As you do, you will find that yourself continuing to evolve into a different more advanced soul. Your desires and intentions develop and diversify as your become more enlightened and more connected with source spirit.

Write more affirmations as you become more confident, and create more abundance in your life, always re-evaluating what it is that you want, because it will constantly change as you progress.

Place importance not on the outcome of your desires but the feelings you experience while you visualise them. You are not separate from what you are manifesting; *you* are the divine energy. There is only one source energy or divine energy in the universe and you are part of that divination. It will happen when you least expect it, although you anticipate it as you have set in motion the attraction for that desire, be a peace knowing that it will come in due course and use your gratitude and appreciation of all things that occur continually. When you are concentrating your attention on appreciation and are patient with yourself and all others, you will find that infinite patience is trust. When you let go of your impatience and expectations you are aligning yourself with Gods force, source sprit, pleasantly all will fall into place and as you become aware of more and more occurrences happening as immediate results start to appear. Be eternally grateful and appreciate each as they appear in your life.

That's why it is best to write down and plan your desires, which some may take a single day or some several long years to achieve, but as you read through previous entries you will notice occurrences you asked for have appeared in your reality, and as you are not dwelling on the outcome, you may not even remember that some of them were on your "list".

Meditate regularly, consume yourself with source energy and allow the universe to unravel as you intended, for it shall manifest itself in accord with your intentions.

"Some books leave us free and some books make us free"

-Ralph Waldo Emerson

Lastly, never stop learning how to develop your mind, body and soul.

"Knowledge is the food of the soul"

-Plato

ABOUT THE AUTHOR

My name is Sarah Davis and I have written the book series "Square Root of Life" to teach you techniques to take control of your life and live however you truly desire.

There is so much I have learnt about life and how I can orchestrate the events and experiences I encounter, so I wanted to share it, empowering others to find an easy path to achieving their goals.

My intention is to teach you "how" to arrange, coordinate, and manipulate the elements that you control in order to achieve your goals, giving you total control of your destiny.

Many readers have been in search for ways to use the Law of Attraction. This book series is written to guide you through the steps of achieving what you want, it has worked for me, so there is no reason it won't work for you.

If you follow the series and habitualise the tasks involved, life is yours for the taking .

Follow me on Facebook; squarerootoflife

or Opt in

www.squarerootoflife.com.au

For the next book in this series; OUT SOON ☺

"Action may not always bring happiness; but

there is no happiness without action"

Benjamin Disraeli

Acknowledgements

I would really like to express my gratitude to many people who have affected my life. I would like to acknowledge these leaders of people, who have had largely influenced various parts of my life, and who have contributed to ultimately provoking new thought patterns and awakening my spiritual nature;

- **Pstr John Hoskin** - Pastor and Youth leader
- **Kristyna Arcarti** - A Beginner's Guide series
- **Regina Thomashauer** - Mama Gena's school of Womanly Arts
- **Neale Donald Walsh** - Conversations with God
- **Dr Wayne W Dyer** - Manifest your Destiny
- **Rhonda Byrne** - The Secret and The Power
- **Pastor Mark Gungor** - Unlocking the Secrets to Life, Love, and Marriage
- **Rev Michael Benard Beckwith** – Fulfilling Your Soul's Potential
- **Bob Proctor** - You Were Born Rich
- **Ester and Jerry Hicks** - The Teachings of Abraham
- **Pam Brossman** - She Experts and Your Millionaire Attitude
- **Michael W Kirton** - Clinical Psychologist, Ted Noff's Assoc
- **Joe Vitale** -Formally assisting me, advising me and certifying me as a Law of Attraction Advanced Practitioner
- My mother
- My late grandmother
- My son

You have all had a huge impact on my life, thank you ☺

"Never let life impede on your ability

to manifest your dreams.

Dig deeper into your dreams

and deeper into yourself

and believe that anything

is possible,

and

make it happen."

Corin Nemec

"Namaste"

My Soul honors your soul

I Honor the place in you where

the entire universe resides.

I honor the light, love and truth,

beauty and peace within you,

because it is also within me.

In sharing these things

We are united, We are the same,

We are one.

1 on 1

Personalised Mentoring

Individual one on one coaching available from the author; Sarah Davis. For individuals who want to improve their results in any and all areas of their life. Everyone is different so sessions are tailored for you specifically based on a proven structure.

Make a committment to yourself, and allow me to guide you through stages to achieve your desires both personally & in business. Sessions are recommended weekly or fortnightly for the best results. I work with adults of all ages including troubled youths, mentoring programs, women entrepreneurs, small business coaching and enlightenment.

- Initial free consultation - an overview of where you're at now, and where you want to be
- One-on-one coaching sessions. Approximately 1 hour each
- Email support
- Phone support - for those moments when you just need to talk to someone for some support and encouragement
- Tools and resources to ensure you can keep yourself on track between coaching sessions and after the coaching process has completed

Areas of Focus

There are 6 main areas that are focused on with clients:

* Business/Career	* Finances
* Relationships	* Health & Fitness
* Emotional State	* Spirituality

If coaching sounds like it might be for you, take the next step and contact me today. You have absolutely nothing to lose and everything to gain by making a call or sending an email. Never be afraid of asking for help.

I have the know-how, knowledge & expertise to excel you in any area that you wish to enhance.

Contact me direct to discuss rates & options.

Sarah Davis

+61 422 648 079

tosarahdavis@gmail.com

2 x #1 Amazon Best Selling Author - Square Root of Life series

Cert. NLP Advanced, practitioner (masters)

Cert. Hypnosis Communicator - Advanced

2 x #1 Amazon Best Selling Author – (Tales 4 Tots)

Best Seller Impact training - Digital Authors academy

Cert. Law of Attraction -Advanced Practitioner

Bachelor of education – EC – Curtin University

Cert IV Business Management

ISBN: 0992416515 (pbk)
ISBN-13: 978-0-9924165-1-5 (pbk)

www.ingramcontent.com/pod-product-compliance
Lightning Source LLC
Chambersburg PA
CBHW060541100426
42742CB00013B/2411